INFERENCES AND DRAWING
CONCLUSIONS PRACTICE PASSAGES
READING COMPREHENSION TEST PREP FOR MIDDLE SCHOOL

by Laura Daly

Contact the author:
writeandreadteacher.com
@writeandreadteacher

TABLE OF CONTENTS

Instructions for Use..4

Inferences Student Guide..5

"The Dog"..6-7

"The Invite"...8-9

"Curfew"..10-11

"Trying Something New"...12-13

"First Day of School"...14-15

"Moving Day"...16-17

"Haircut"...18-19

"The Movie"..20-21

"The Football Game"...22-23

"The Dress"...24-25

"The Journal"...26-27

"A New Restaurant"..28-29

Answer Keys...30-34

INSTRUCTIONS FOR USE

This workbook contains 12 different fiction passages to teach students how to read closely and make inferences. The passages in this book are in order of difficulty. The first passage is the easiest, and the last passage is the most difficult. With passages at different levels, you can build your way to more challenging texts as a class or use different passages for differentiated instruction to fit students' needs.

The following page is an inferences guide for students. It defines inferences and provides examples. This is a good resource for students to read over before they begin working on the practice passages.

Answer keys can be found at the back of the book. Keep in mind that they are sample answers. Student answers will vary some.

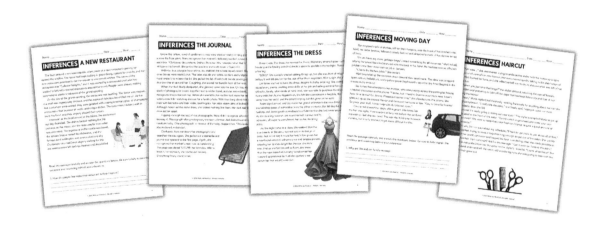

INFERENCES AND DRAWING CONCLUSIONS STUDENT GUIDE

When you make an inference, you are coming to a conclusion using evidence and reasoning.

Let's look at some examples.

PASSAGE	INFERENCE
"These are still warm from the oven. Try one," Kate offered, holding the tray out to her friend. "Thank you," Matt replied biting into a cookie with a crunch. He made a sound of approval as he chewed. Suddenly, he stopped chewing. Kate thought he looked a bit flushed. "What's in these?" he asked with wide eyes.	Although the passage doesn't say that Matt has a food allergy, readers can infer that he has one. He suddenly stopped eating even though he enjoyed the taste. He looked red in the face, and he asked about the ingredients.
DJ tiptoed into the house. He peeked into the kitchen. It was empty. This was his chance. He headed straight for the garbage can. He pulled his math test from his backpack and quietly pushed it to the bottom of the full can. "DJ, is that you?" his mom called from upstairs. "How did your math test go today, honey?" "I think it went well, Mom. The teacher hasn't graded it yet. We might not get it back until next week," he called back, hoping she'd forget about it.	Although the passage doesn't say how DJ did on his test, readers can infer that he failed it. He threw it away and pushed it to the bottom of the garbage. He also lied to his mom about it not being graded yet and hoped she would forget about it.

INFERENCES THE DOG

Joe was headed home from practice when he heard the smallest whimper from a nearby bush. Curious, he poked his head in and saw a small, shivering puppy huddled under it. Its fur was matted, and it was skin and bones. When it saw Joe, its eyes lit up, tail wagging. Joe coaxed the puppy out and started looking it over, worried about injuries and wondering who it might belong to. The puppy didn't have a collar, and while Joe wasn't allowed to have pets, he couldn't bear to leave it on the street. "I'm going to call you Max," he told it, cradling it carefully in his arms.

Joe finished walking home and slid Max in his jacket as he walked into the house. He quickly greeted his mom then hurried toward the stairs, hoping to make it safely to his room before his mom noticed the puppy. Right as Joe hit the stairs, Max started whining. "What was that?" his mom asked.

"Umm, just my phone. New ringtone," he replied quickly as he bolted up the stairs.

Once inside his room, he put Max down and tried to figure out what to do. He'd never had a dog before, so he didn't know what it needed to eat, and he certainly didn't know how to take care of its matted fur. As he stood there wondering what to do, the puppy peed on the floor. "Max! Oh, no!"

Joe ran downstairs for paper towels and cleaner. "Whoa, what's the rush?" his mom asked.

"Um, I spilled something. Just want to get it cleaned up," Joe stammered, inching back toward the stairs.

"Do you need help?"

"Nope, I'm good," he almost shouted as he ran back up the stairs.

As he finished cleaning up his carpet, Joe realized he needed to figure out something for Max to eat. He looked it up online and saw he could feed Max rice and chicken. He headed back downstairs and started rummaging through the cabinets looking for the rice. "Can I help you find something?" his mom asked curiously.

"Where's the rice?"

"Rice? Why do you need rice?"

"Just hungry. Maybe some chicken, too."

His mom got the rice out of the right cabinet and pulled some chicken out of the fridge. "I don't think you've ever requested rice, let alone made it yourself," his mom remarked lightly.

"What are you going to season it with?"

"Season it? I'm just going to eat it plain," Joe said, trying to sound excited about it.

"I see. I'll leave you to it," his mom replied, a bit confused.

Joe took the finished food back to Max, who happily ate some and fell asleep. Joe took the opportunity to run the dishes downstairs, and when he came back, he couldn't find Max. He started moving things and digging through his clothes, but he had no luck. He had no idea where Max could have gone!

Joe slowly went back downstairs to find his mom. "I need help," he said quietly.

"With the puppy you snuck in the house?" she asked.

Read the passage carefully and answer the questions below. Be sure to fully explain the evidence and reasoning behind your inferences.

1. Why does Joe bring the puppy home?

_____

_____

2. Explain the evidence and reasoning behind your previous answer.

_____

_____

_____

_____

3. How did Joe's mom know about the puppy?

_____

_____

4. Explain the evidence and reasoning behind your previous answer.

_____

_____

_____

INFERENCES THE INVITE

As Mia approached her locker after algebra, she saw that Lily and Sarah were already waiting for her. She flipped through the combination lock quickly and pulled her locker door open. "Hi, ladies. Ready for lunch?" Her friends, deeply engrossed in something in Lily's hand, didn't respond. "Uh, hello? What are you two looking at?"

Startled, Sarah jumped. "Oh, hey. We were just talking about Jake's party. We got invites before chemistry."

"What?" choked Mia. Jake was the most popular guy in their grade, and his parties were epic.

"Wait. You didn't get invited?" asked Lily.

Mia's cheeks reddened with embarrassment. "Oh, yeah. I did. I just meant what about it? What were you talking about? That's all."

"Oh, thank goodness because we all have to go to this party. Sarah and I are going to see who else is invited, okay? We'll meet you in the cafeteria." Without waiting for a response, the two girls bounded away down the hall and disappeared into a group of girls wearing cheerleading uniforms.

Mia turned her back from the hall and faced her open locker. A single tear ran down her cheek, and she quickly wiped it away with the sleeve of her shirt.

Read the passage carefully and answer the questions below. Be sure to fully explain the evidence and reasoning behind your inferences.

1. What can you infer about Mia and the party?

_____

_____

_____

INFERENCES THE INVITE

2. Explain the evidence and reasoning behind your previous answer.

_____

_____

_____

_____

_____

3. How is Mia feeling?

_____

_____

_____

4. Explain the evidence and reasoning behind your previous answer.

_____

_____

_____

_____

_____

Name _____ Date _____ Hour_____

INFERENCES CURFEW

It was a typical Friday night for 17-year-old Sarah. She had spent the evening hanging out with her friends, playing card games, and eating junk food.

Panic set in as she checked her phone and saw that it was 11:45 p.m. Her curfew was at midnight, and her parents had been very clear about it. If she was even a minute late, she figured she would be grounded for a week.

"Oh, no!" Sarah exclaimed to her friends. "I've gotta run; I can't be late for curfew." She put her cards down and started to get up from the table.

"Come on, Sarah. It's fine. You can't leave until the game is over. It's your turn," her friend said nonchalantly, not worried at all. "Just call your parents and explain."

"They won't care. My curfew is midnight, and it's non-negotiable. Sorry guys, you'll have to finish the game without me." Sarah waved goodbye and headed to the door. She stopped when she heard her friends grumbling, wondering how they were going to finish the game without her. She hovered by the door, debating whether she should give in and keep playing the game but decided she'd rather her friends be a little upset instead of her parents.

She walked quickly down the street, headed toward home. It wasn't a long walk, but she was cutting it close. She sped up, continuously checking her phone as she watched the time tick closer to midnight. She turned on her street and started running, trying to beat the clock.

Breathless and sweating, Sarah fumbled with her keys and finally managed to unlock the door. As she stepped inside, she could see her parents sitting in the living room, waiting for her.

"Sarah, do you know what time it is?" her mother asked. Sarah looked at her phone. 12:02 a.m.

"I'm sorry, Mom. I lost track of time," Sarah replied, trying to catch her breath. "We were in the middle of a game when I realized how late it had gotten."

"Were you running?" her dad asked.

"Yes, I left before we finished the game, but it wasn't early enough."

Her parents looked at each other and sighed. Sarah braced herself for the lecture. "We're glad you tried to get home on time, but please don't run in the dark; it's not safe.

INFERENCES CURFEW

Next time, pay more attention to the time. Tonight, since you tried so hard to get home, we'll give you a pass. We're going to bed. Goodnight." With a quick hug, her parents headed up the stairs to bed. Sarah stood in the doorway, dazed, trying to figure out what had just happened.

Read the passage carefully and answer the questions below. Be sure to fully explain the evidence and reasoning behind your inferences.

1. How do Sarah's friends feel about her leaving?

_____

_____

_____

2. Explain the evidence and reasoning behind your previous answer.

_____

_____

_____

_____

_____

3. How does Sarah feel after her parents don't ground her?

_____

_____

_____

4. Explain the evidence and reasoning behind your previous answer.

_____

_____

_____

_____

INFERENCES TRYING SOMETHING NEW

Gus and the guys spent their days playing video games, so engrossed in their virtual world, they didn't bother with much outside of it other than school.

One morning at school, a new kid, Trevor, joined the class. Gus overhead Trevor telling the class about all the different things he liked to do: reading, hiking, and especially rock climbing. "Wow, that kind of sounds like fun," Gus thought to himself, but then his friend started asking about the next level to beat. Gus forgot about Trevor.

On the bus ride home, Gus noticed Trevor again. Trevor was telling someone else about rock climbing, and Gus found himself listening instead of playing the game on his phone. Trevor noticed Gus listening and asked, "You ever climb, man?"

"Oh, no," Gus replied, "I'm more of an indoor guy."

"Dude, I do most of my climbing indoors. I haven't been since I moved, but I heard this town's got an indoor climbing gym. I'm going to check it out tomorrow if anyone wants to join." Gus shook his head no and looked back at his phone, ignoring Trevor for the rest of the ride.

That night, Gus lay in bed thinking about rock climbing. He'd never done anything like that before, and it sounded exciting. The way Trevor talked about it made Gus want to try it, but there was no way he could go. He didn't know anything about climbing! And what would his friends think? Gus turned in over in bed, conflicted about what to do.

Gus was off kilter at school all morning the next day. He barely listened to his friends as they talked about their plans for the game, instead Googling the place Trevor was planning to go after school. He started looking up other things, too, like "basics of indoor rock climbing" and "how do you rock climb?" His friends made plans to play the game after dinner that night.

As school ended, Gus made up his mind. He ran to the bus to find Trevor.

INFERENCES TRYING SOMETHING NEW

Read the passage carefully and answer the questions below. Be sure to fully explain the evidence and reasoning behind your inferences.

1. What conflicting emotions does Gus feel about indoor rock climbing?

_____

_____

_____

2. Explain the evidence and reasoning behind your previous answer.

_____

_____

_____

_____

_____

_____

3. What does Gus decide to do?

_____

_____

4. Explain the evidence and reasoning behind your previous answer.

_____

_____

_____

_____

_____

INFERENCES FIRST DAY OF SCHOOL

It was the first day of school, and Emily was feeling a mixture of emotions. She had just moved to the town and was starting at a new school. They'd moved after new student orientation, so she hadn't met any students or had a chance to walk through her schedule.

Emily woke up early, put on her new school uniform, and packed her bag with all the necessary supplies. Her mother had made breakfast, but Emily could only stomach half a piece of toast—her stomach was in knots.

As she entered the school gates, she was greeted by a bustling crowd of students, all looking just as nervous as she was. Emily made her way to the main building, following the signs that led her to her first class, English. She took a seat in the back, hoping to blend in and not draw too much attention to herself. She looked around at the other students, wondering who might be friendly, when she noticed a girl coming down the row, smiling at her. Just as Emily went to introduce herself, the bell rang, and the teacher demanded their attention.

The day passed in a bit of a blur until lunch. As she entered the cafeteria, Emily scanned the room quickly, trying to figure out where to sit. She didn't recognize anyone from any of her classes, and every table had at least one person sitting at it. She started walking slowly through the room, trying to make eye contact with different students to ask about sitting with them. No one looked up. She was almost to the back of the cafeteria, and her heart started racing. What should she do?

Just as she felt tears starting to well up, the girl from English class waved her over. "Hey, you're in my English class, right? Emma? We've got an extra chair here."

Emily sank into the chair. "Close, it's Emily. Hi."

"I'm Kayla, and this is Tee," the girl said, motioning to the other girl sitting next to her. Emily smiled at both girls, grateful to have found someone to sit with.

INFERENCES FIRST DAY OF SCHOOL

Read the passage carefully and answer the questions below. Be sure to fully explain the evidence and reasoning behind your inferences.

1. How does Emily feel on the morning of her first day of school?

_____

_____

_____

2. Explain the evidence and reasoning behind your previous answer.

_____

_____

_____

_____

_____

_____

3. How do Emily's emotions change while in the cafeteria?

_____

_____

_____

4. Explain the evidence and reasoning behind your previous answer.

_____

_____

_____

_____

_____

_____

INFERENCES MOVING DAY

Gia dropped a pile of clothes, still on their hangers, into the trunk of her mother's car. Matt, her older brother, followed closely behind and dropped a stack of his clothes on top of hers.

"Do we have any more garbage bags? I need something for all my shoes," Matt asked, wiping the sweat from his forehead with the back of his hand. He had become an efficient packer since their mom lost her job in January.

"Check the kitchen table," Gia replied.

Matt bounded up the concrete steps toward their apartment. The door was propped open with a cinderblock, and a yellow paper haphazardly taped to the front flapped in the breeze as he entered.

Gia turned her attention to her mother, who was pacing across the parking lot having a heated discussion on the phone. "I know, but I need to borrow your truck now. I don't have time to wait for Jimmy. Please just come now," she pleaded into the phone. She glanced up as she passed the car and furrowed her brow at Gia. "Gia, no time for breaks! Go pack your stuff. I need help with the kitchen soon."

Gia turned toward the steps with a groan. She knew her mother was right. They needed to be gone before the landlord showed up, but she was tired. This was the third time in seven months, but it only seemed to get more difficult for Gia.

Read the passage carefully and answer the questions below. Be sure to fully explain the evidence and reasoning behind your inferences.

1. Why are Gia and her family moving?

_____

_____

_____

INFERENCES MOVING DAY

2. Explain the evidence and reasoning behind your previous answer.

_____

_____

_____

_____

_____

_____

3. How does Gia feel about moving?

_____

_____

_____

4. Explain the evidence and reasoning behind your previous answer.

_____

_____

_____

_____

_____

_____

INFERENCES HAIRCUT

"Oh wow..." she stammered, trying to smile as the stylist held the mirror up to give Maria a full view of her new haircut. Her eyes moved quickly taking in the short wisps of hair that framed her face, and she willed herself not to cry as she saw what was left of her long hair.

"Don't you just love the bangs?" the stylist chirped, brushing the hair off Maria's shoulders and preparing to take off the cape that had kept Maria dry and free of hair during the haircut.

"Yeah," Maria replied half-heartedly, looking frantically for anything about her hair she could compliment. "I really like the color," she finally said, hoping it came out more enthusiastic than she felt.

"I know! It's really going to bring out your eyes." The stylist prompted Maria to get up and headed to the front of the salon. "Do you want to go ahead and book your next appointment? We want to keep that color fresh and bangs require a good amount of maintenance."

"Oh, um, I'm not sure about my schedule; I'll have to get back to you about all of that," Maria replied, trying to keep it together long enough to get out of the salon. She quickly handed her credit card over and tapped her foot, wondering what she could possibly do about her hair. Do I complain? Ask for the manager? Can it even be fixed at this point?

Maria was pulled from her thoughts by the stylist's cheerful, "You're all set here!" She gave a weak smile and left the salon, still wondering how she was going to deal with this until her hair grew out.

INFERENCES HAIRCUT

Read the passage carefully and answer the questions below. Be sure to fully explain the evidence and reasoning behind your inferences.

1. What can readers infer about Maria's haircut?

_____

_____

_____

2. Explain the evidence and reasoning behind your previous answer.

_____

_____

_____

_____

_____

_____

3. What does the stylist think about Maria's haircut?

_____

_____

_____

4. Explain the evidence and reasoning behind your previous answer.

_____

_____

_____

_____

_____

_____

INFERENCES THE MOVIE

Carmen waited outside the theater for friends, shifting back and forth from one foot to the other. She pulled her coat tightly around her, scanning the people walking up to the doors, hoping she'd see one of them soon. She checked her phone for what felt like the thousandth time and anxiously did the math on how much time was left before the movie started. Still no messages, and the movie started in just 10 minutes. She debated whether she should buy her own ticket and go inside to get snacks, but she didn't want to miss her friends. Carmen finally spotted them and quickly waved so they would see her.

"Sorry we're late. We decided we wanted to see a different movie, and it doesn't start for another 15 minutes," Hannah said.

"Yeah, we want to see that new horror movie everyone's talking about," Morgan agreed.

"You could have told me you changed your minds. I'm in the mood for that comedy we talked about," Carmen said, annoyed, "I've been waiting here forever."

"We figured you wouldn't mind," Morgan replied nonchalantly, as they all moved to the ticket line. "You never have strong opinions about the movies we see, and I heard that comedy isn't very funny. Besides, everyone's going to be talking about this horror movie at school next week."

Carmen watched the line as they got closer to the ticket booth, trying to decide whether to go along with her friends' plan. She chewed on her lip, wondering about the horror movie. She had been looking forward to the comedy; she loved the star in everything he was in, but she normally wouldn't care that much. This was different though. Would she be able to make it through the movie without embarrassing herself? It was time. She bought her ticket and headed to the theater with her friends.

Carmen started imagining all the ways this could go wrong. As the previews ended, Carmen sat on her hands, the dark theater only amplifying her feelings. With the first jump scare, Carmen screamed and covered her eyes.

INFERENCES THE MOVIE

Read the passage carefully and answer the questions below. Be sure to fully explain the evidence and reasoning behind your inferences.

1. How does Carmen feel while waiting for her friends?

_____

_____

_____

2. Explain the evidence and reasoning behind your previous answer.

_____

_____

_____

_____

_____

_____

3. How does Carmen feel about the new movie her friends picked?

_____

_____

_____

4. Explain the evidence and reasoning behind your previous answer.

_____

_____

_____

_____

_____

_____

INFERENCES THE FOOTBALL GAME

"Isn't this exciting? I know you're a huge football fan, so you must have been looking forward to this game all season," Anthony bellowed over the cheers of the crowd.

"Absolutely," Troy agreed smiling widely at Anthony.

The Bulldogs were playing their rivals, the Longhorns, in a game that would determine who would be moving on to the state semi finals. From the crowd in the bleachers, Troy guessed half the town had shown up to support the team. He and Anthony had gotten there half an hour early, and they struggled to find seats. They had managed to squeeze into a row between a group of freshman girls with face paint and pompoms and a burly old man in an ancient jersey two sizes too small.

Troy had picked the seat next to the muscular old man and regretted that decision. Every time the Bulldogs made a touchdown, the old man's aggressive clapping would send Troy crashing into Anthony. At least he didn't have to deal with pompoms in the face like his friend though.

Suddenly, the commentator shouted "Touchdown Bulldogs!" over the loudspeaker causing Troy to jump, startled. He took a deep breath and straightened the Bulldogs jersey he had borrowed from his brother. The fans in the bleachers cheered and stomped their feet sending reverberations through the stands, and Troy closed his eyes trying to fight the nausea creeping in.

"Whoa. Did you see that interception?" Anthony yelled over the crowd.

Troy opened his eyes to find Anthony standing and clapping. "What's an interception?" Troy asked.

"Like you don't know. You're funny, man," he replied clamping a hand on Troy's shoulder.

"Yeah, sure," he agreed. His eyes searched beyond the sea of blue in the stands to the scoreboard to see how much time remained. He sighed.

INFERENCES THE FOOTBALL GAME

Read the passage carefully and answer the questions below. Be sure to fully explain the evidence and reasoning behind your inferences.

1. How does Troy feel about football and being at the game?

_____

_____

_____

2. Explain the evidence and reasoning behind your previous answer.

_____

_____

_____

_____

_____

3. What can you infer about the friendship between Anthony and Troy?

_____

_____

_____

4. Explain the evidence and reasoning behind your previous answer.

_____

_____

_____

_____

_____

Name _____ Date _____ Hour_____

INFERENCES THE DRESS

There it was. The dress she needed for Prom. Shimmery emerald green with intricate beading and a flowing train that made it seem to sparkle in the sunlight. Then she saw the price tag.

"$300!" She mentally started adding things up, but she was short of what she'd need to buy it and still pay her for the rest of her Prom expenses. With a sigh, she left the shop.

Lily knew she had to have the dress, despite its hefty price tag. She scrimped and saved every penny, working extra shifts at her job and selling some of her old clothes to afford it. Finally, after weeks of hard work, she was able to purchase the dress and bring it home with her. As she slipped it on, she felt like a princess in a fairytale, the fabric flowing away from her waist, and the color bringing out the green in her eyes.

Prom night arrived, and Lily made her grand entrance in the new dress, turning heads and eliciting gasps of admiration from the other students. She felt like the belle of the ball, twirling and dancing with a newfound confidence that she had never experienced before. As the evening wore on, she found herself surrounded by admirers, all eager to compliment her on her stunning attire.

As the night came to a close, Lily realized that the true beauty of the dress was not just in its design or color, but in the way it made her feel. It had given her a newfound sense of self-assurance and empowerment, allowing her to shine bright like the star she truly was. And as she bid farewell to Prom, she knew that the new dress had not only transformed her outward appearance but had also ignited a fire within her that would never dim.

INFERENCES THE DRESS

Read the passage carefully and answer the questions below. Be sure to fully explain the evidence and reasoning behind your inferences.

1. How does Lily feel when she leaves the shop without the dress?

_____

_____

_____

2. Explain the evidence and reasoning behind your previous answer.

_____

_____

_____

_____

_____

_____

3. How does Lily feel wearing the dress at Prom?

_____

_____

_____

4. Explain the evidence and reasoning behind your previous answer.

_____

_____

_____

_____

_____

_____

INFERENCES THE JOURNAL

Under the rafters, rows of cardboard boxes were stacked neatly on long planks laid across the floor joists. Nora recognized her mother's delicately swirled cursive labeling each box. "Christmas decorations. Dishes. Personal. Hm. I wonder what that is," she whispered to herself. She pulled the box free and knelt down in front of it.

With the box sitting in front of her, she realized the lid was taped closed. None of the other boxes were sealed shut. The tape was old and brittle, so Nora easily slipped her hand under it to release the lid. She pulled the lid off with both hands sending a cloud of dust into the air around her. Coughing, she waved her hand in front of her face.

When the dust finally dissipated, she glanced down into the box. On top, she found a stack of photographs bound together with a rubber band, and she immediately recognized the picture on top. When she was little, her mother had made her and her sisters wear frilly matching dresses for a family photo. With their long blond hair pulled back with barrettes and their wide, toothy grins, her older sisters almost looked like twins. Although Nora had the same dress, she looked nothing like them. Her dark hair and wide nose set her apart.

Flipping through the rest of the photographs, Nora didn't recognize who she was looking at. Photograph after photograph, she saw a slender, dark-haired woman holding a newborn baby. One photograph, a closeup of the baby, stopped her. "This looks like me," she muttered in disbelief.

Confused, Nora set down the photographs and searched the box again. She pulled out a leatherbound journal and opened to the first page. Again, she recognized her mother's neat cursive handwriting. The page was dated 11/17/98, her birthday. With a knot in her stomach, she continued reading. Everything finally made sense.

INFERENCES THE JOURNAL

Read the passage carefully and answer the questions below. Be sure to fully explain the evidence and reasoning behind your inferences.

1. Where is Nora?

_____

_____

_____

2. Explain the evidence and reasoning behind your previous answer.

_____

_____

_____

_____

_____

_____

3. What does Nora discover?

_____

_____

_____

4. Explain the evidence and reasoning behind your previous answer.

_____

_____

_____

_____

_____

_____

Name _____ Date _____ Hour_____

INFERENCES A NEW RESTAURANT

The buzz around town was palpable when news of a new restaurant opening up spread like wildfire. The town had been lacking in good dining options for a while, and this new restaurant promised to be the answer to everyone's wishes. The name of the restaurant was "Culinary Delights," and it was owned by a renowned chef who had worked in Michelin-starred restaurants around the world. People were already making reservations weeks in advance of the grand opening.

On the day of the grand opening, the restaurant was bustling. The decor was elegant, the staff was impeccably dressed, and the aroma of delicious food filled the air. As the first customers were seated, they were greeted with a complimentary glass of champagne and a menu that boasted of exotic and unique dishes. The customers couldn't wait to taste the food, and they eagerly placed their orders.

However, as the food arrived at the tables, the excitement quickly dwindled. The dishes looked nothing like the pictures on the menu, and the taste was far from what was promised. The expensive truffle risotto was bland, the lobster bisque tasted like dishwater, and the famous beef wellington was overcooked and dry. Customers who had been eagerly waiting for this experience were left feeling cheated and dissatisfied.

Read the passage carefully and answer the questions below. Be sure to fully explain the evidence and reasoning behind your inferences.

1. How do people feel about the restaurant before it opens?

_____

_____

_____

INFERENCES A NEW RESTAURANT

2. Explain the evidence and reasoning behind your previous answer.

_____
_____
_____
_____
_____
_____

3. How do people feel about the restaurant after eating there?

_____
_____
_____

4. Explain the evidence and reasoning behind your previous answer.

_____
_____
_____
_____
_____
_____

ANSWER KEY

"The Dog" pages 6-7
1. He feels for the puppy because it looks so bad, and it was excited to see Joe.
2. The puppy's fur is matted. It is skinny and has no collar. When it sees Joe, its eye light up and the tail wags. It also says he "couldn't bear to leave it."
3. Joe was acting strangely when he got home. It means cracks.
4. Joe needed cleaning supplies for his room and wanted to cook something he's never asked to eat. He didn't want to season it, so it would taste bland. He also said the dog whine was a new ringtone.

"The Invite" pages 8-9
1. Readers can infer that Mia wasn't invited to the party.
2. If she had been invited to the party, she probably would have known what her friends were looking at. Also, she blushes when her friends ask if she was invited.
3. She's embarrassed and upset.
4. She's probably embarrassed because she didn't tell her friends the truth. She's also upset about it and cries when her friends leave.

"Curfew" pages 10-11
1. They're annoyed she's leaving without finishing the game.
2. They ask her to stay to finish the game and call her parents to explain. She also hears them grumbling as she's leaving.
3. She's surprised.
4. She braces herself for a lecture, and she's "dazed, trying to figure out what had just happened" when she doesn't get a punishment.

"Trying Something New" pages 12-13
1. He thinks it sounds cool and would be excited to try it, but he is nervous.
2. Gus keeps listening to Trevor and thinks about it while he's in bed. He's nervous because he's never done anything like it before and is worried what his friends will think.
3. He decides to go rock climbing with Trevor.
4. After school, he runs to the bus to find Trevor. He wouldn't need to find Trevor if he wasn't going with him.

"First Day of School" pages 14-15
1. She feels nervous.
2. It's a new school in a new town, and she missed orientation. It also says, "her stomach was in knots."
3. She's uncomfortable when she first walks in, but she is happy after finding somewhere to sit.
4. She's uncomfortable because she doesn't recognize anyone, so she doesn't know where to sit. Her heart was racing and she "felt tears starting to well up." Later, she's happy because Kayla invites her to sit down, and she "smiled" and feels "grateful."

"Moving Day" pages 16-17
1. Gia and her family are being evicted from their apartment.
2. The passage says her mom has been out of work. This also doesn't seem to be a planned move because they don't have boxes or a truck lined up. They're putting clothes directly into the trunk, and Matt is going to use trash bags to hold his things. Something is taped to their front door. It could be an eviction notice.
3. Gia isn't happy about the move.
4. She groans when her mom tells her to pack. The passage also says the Gia was tired and the moves were getting more difficult for her.

"Haircut" pages 18-19
1. We can infer that she didn't get the haircut she asked the stylist for.
2. She clearly doesn't like her haircut, and she wouldn't have asked for something she didn't like. She stammers and struggles to come up with something positive to say to the stylist. She also has to fight back tears and wonders if she should complain.
3. She thinks it's a great haircut.
4. Her attitude is positive and cheerful, and she talks about how the color will bring out Maria's eyes.

ANSWER KEY

"The Movie" pages 20-21
1. She feels anxious about them being late and missing part of the movie.
2. She's shifting back and forth and keeps checking her phone. She also debates about just buying a ticket herself.
3. She doesn't want to see it. She's nervous about watching a horror movie.
4. She complains about how she wanted to see the comedy and is worried about embarrassing herself. Then, during the movie, she sits on her hands before screaming and covering her eyes.

"The Football Game" pages 22-23
1. He doesn't like being there, and he isn't a football fan.
2. He isn't really watching the game, and he doesn't like the crowded bleachers. He's uncomfortable and feeling sick. He also doesn't know what an interception is, and he's wearing a borrowed jersey. A real football fan would know the game and have their own fan clothing.
3. They probably haven't known each other long, or they aren't close friends.
4. Anthony seems to think that Troy really likes football and that he's excited to be at the game. That isn't case, so he must not know him very well.

"The Dress" pages 24-25
1. She's disappointed.
2. She sighs when she leaves and then decides to scrimp and save and work extra shifts to be able to buy it.
3. She feels beautiful and confident.
4. People give her lots of compliments, she feels like "the belle of the ball," and she got to "shine bright like the star she truly was."

"The Journal" pages 26-27
1. She's in her parents' attic.
2. It's a dusty room with rafters, so it's an attic. It's probably her parents' attic because her mother's handwriting is on all the boxes, and she doesn't know what's inside them.
3. She was adopted into this family.
4. She doesn't look like her family members. She also found pictures of an unknown woman holding her when she was a baby and a journal that her mom started when she was born. The journal probably reveals the adoption process.

"A New Restaurant" pages 28-29
1. Everyone is excited to eat there.
2. There's a buzz about the restaurant, and the chef has worked around the world. The restaurant is also "bustling" on the first night which means people wanted to try it.
3. They're disappointed.
4. Nothing looks or tastes like it's supposed. They leave feeling "cheating and dissatisfied."

Connect with the author:
writeandreadteacher.com
@writeandreadteacher

WRITE
AND
READ

Made in the USA
Las Vegas, NV
18 November 2024